J.N. Culver

Loyal Mountaineers

Vol. 3

J.N. Culver

Loyal Mountaineers
Vol. 3

ISBN/EAN: 9783337289607

Printed in Europe, USA, Canada, Australia, Japan

Cover: Foto ©ninafisch / pixelio.de

More available books at **www.hansebooks.com**

LOYAL MOUNTAINEERS:

OR,

The Guerrilla's Doom.

—◦◊◦—

A WAR DRAMA,

DESCRIPTIVE OF THE HARDSHIPS, SUFFERINGS, AND BRAVE ENDURANCE
OF THE UNIONISTS OF EAST TENNESSEE.

FOUNDED ON FACTS.

By

J. N. CULVER,

Under the Auspices of Baldy Smith Post No. 20, Dept. of Vt.,

AND

RESPECTFULLY DEDICATED TO THE GRAND ARMY OF THE REPUBLIC.

—◦◊◦—

St. Albans, Vt.:
E. A. MORTON, PRINTER.
1872.

Cast of Characters.

UNIONISTS.

MR. MARKS.....................................A Tennessee Farmer.
WM. MARKS.............................Son of Mr. Marks, in Union army.
WALTER GREENWOOD.......................................Union Spy.
JOHN STEEL..Union Soldier.
ROBERT DAVIS.."
CHARLEY BATES..."
PAT O'DOHERTY..."
OLD BEN...Contraband.
SAM HANNIBAL..."
COL. BARKER.........................Commanding Union Regiment.
CAPT. DUNBAR.......................   "   "   Company.
    ADJUTANT, OFFICERS AND SOLDIERS.
ALICE MARKS...........................Daughter of Mr. Marks
CLARA STEEL..............................Sister to Fred Steel.
WIDOW POWERS...............................Tennessee Lady.
MARY POWERS..............................Mrs. Powers' Daughter.

CONFEDERATES.

FRED STEEL.....................................Chief of Guerrillas.
SAM SMITH...Guerrilla.
TOM JONES.."
JOE BLAKE (Greenwood in disguise).......................... "
ABRAHAM ALLEN (Conscripted).......................Rebel Guard.
GEORGE MACK... "

COSTUMES.

Mr. Marks—1st. Hunting, with blanket, gun, &c. 2d. Private. 3d. Prison. 4th. Private.

Wm. Marks—Private soldier.

Walter Greenwood—1st. Disguised as Guerrilla. 2d. Captain. 3d. 4th. Prison. Disguised. 5th. Captain.

John Steel—Prison.

Robert Davis—1st. Prison. 2d. Private. 3d. Prison. 4th. Private.

Charley Bates—1st. Prison. 2d. Private.

Pat O'Doherty—Private.

Old Ben—Prison.

Sam Hannibal.—1st. Plantation. 2d. Soldier.

Col. Barker, Capt. Dunbar, Adjutant, &c., equipped according to regulations.

Alice Marks—1st. Mourning. 2d. Traveling. 3d. Bridal.

Clara Steel—1st Mourning. 2d. Traveling.

Mary Powers, Widow Powers—Home.

Fred Steel—Guerrilla Colonel (Light Gray).

Sam Smith—   "   Captain.   "

Tom Jones—   "   Private.   "

Joe Blake—   "   "   "

Abraham Allen.—Private C. S. A.

Geo. Mack—Sergeant C. S. A.

LOYAL MOUNTAINEERS;

OR,

THE GUERRILLA'S DOOM.

———◆·●·◆———

ACT I.

SCENE FIRST.

Wood or Mountain Scene—Fred Steel and his Gang of Guerrillas discovered Playing Cards, Smoking, and Drinking —"We'll Not Go Home Till Morning."

FRED STEEL.—Well, boys, we must hurry up our talking; for you know I am off before light to-morrow morning.

TOM JONES.—Yes, Colonel, I know we have got to part with you; but we must have a sort of good-by spree, you know.

FRED STEEL.—Yes, boys, I am going to leave you; but, if I don't like it at Libby, I shall come back again. Now, before we break up, I want you to elect a new Captain. I want you to put in a man who won't be afraid to hear a woman yell, either; for sometimes they have tried to bother us when we have been sort of looking over their houses. I have thought Sam would make a good one. What do the rest of you think?

All of the the Guerrillas call for Sam Smith, Captain Smith, &c., &c.

SAM SMITH.—I don't know what to say, boys ; I am no speech maker ; but I didn't onc't think you would appint me Capum ; there is men here as has got more larnin' than I has, but, if you want me, I never will ask one on yer ter go where I won't.

All the Guerrillas exclaim : "Good, good ! Hurrah for Captain Sam."—All cheer.

FRED STEEL.—We have been together, boys, for over two years, and there is not a man here but what can count his stamps by the thousand ; and, while we have been helping ourselves, we have been supporting the "Bonnie Blue Flag." I received a letter of commendation from Gen. John Morgan, to-day, with my Colonel's commission.

He says that our company has been the most successful of any under his command, and that he wishes he had more such men. So don't let a chance slip to strike a blow for Southern rights. To be sure, we have suffered—all brave soldiers must. We have lost many good men by these so-called "Loyal Mountaineers," who are nothing but cowards at best, and thanks be to Capt. Sam Smith's Rangers that the country is rid of some of them.

SAM SMITH.—Only one man now lives that I really dread, and that is Old Marks. I think I've seen him onc't, but don't know him. I seen an old man with long white hair and whiskers, and if I had had my gun, I would have known, sure.

FRED STEEL.—Sam, I don't want Old Marks killed. You know we went to his house in the night, and got about ten thousand dollars in gold, put the old woman and Charlie out of the way, and 1 have Alice down to Widow Powers'. We burnt up the old man's house, and I guess on the whole he has got his pay for his Yankee talk.

Sam Smith.—Yes, I know all that; and we thought the old man was dead, too; but here he has been prowling round like a hyena, and has murdered sixteen of our best boys. I think he ought to be put out of the way.

Fred Steel.—You are Captain now, and will do just as you choose after I am gone; but I wish we could take him prisoner—and then don't you see I could MAKE him give his consent to my marrying Alice?

Sam Smith.—There is something to that, Colonel; and I will promise you that we will take him alive, if possible; but if I get sight of him, he's my prisoner, dead or alive.

Tom Jones.—Come, come, we must be moving, or we shan't get a chance to make an honest dollar tonight.

Fred Steel.—I know, Tom, but I want to chat with you a little before I go, and we want to drink Captain Sam's health, too. You know this Yankee whisky is tiptop. How that chap did bellow when I popped him over and took his team and barrel of whisky.

Tom Jones.—Good whisky, too; pity there weren't two barrels of it. And now I propose we drink first Col. Fred Steel's good health, and next Capt. Sam Smith's—and then we will proceed to close. All ready.

All take their canteens or flasks.

Here's to Col. Fred Steel, who has proved true to his name while our Captain for the last two years.

All drink.

Now here is to Sam Smith, who's our Captain to be, While we scout over the mountains in East Tennesse.

All drink.

Here is to Alice Marks, our Colonel's brightest shil-
ling,
And he'll surely marry her, if the Old Man is willing.

FRED STEEL.—Now, boys, here is one for you. May you all prove as true to your new Captain as you have to me.

Drinks.

Since our company has been organized we have supported ourselves from the Yankee army. When we first started there were only six of us. Now we have over one hundred. We have taken all of our horses from the Yankee army, and nearly all we have came from them. Gen. Morgan writes me that there are twenty-three hundred men in the whole regiment, and all that he has ever had from the South was twenty-seven army saddles—his horses, clothing, arms and ammunition having been taken from the Yankees.

SAM SMITH.—Colonel, do you know where Old Marks is now?

FRED STEEL.—No, I can not tell, but I think he is over the other side of the mountain. I am going down to Widow Powers' to-night to try and persuade Alice to go to Richmond with me. How like

a fool she behaves. She shall be my wife, sooner or later.

TOM JONES,—O, Colonel, what's the use; you don't want any wife, and she is bound to have that Spy, Walter Greenwood, any way, and she can't marry you both.

FRED STEEL.—Greenwood is far from here in the Army of the Potomac, and Alice Marks can not see him. If he is brought to Libby while I am in command, won't I have some sport? [Looks at his watch.] Well, boys, we must part. I am bound to see Alice before I go. Here, Captain [Gives him his Revolver], take this as a present.

SAM SMITH.—Thank'e, Colonel, I'll try and make good usn on't. I suppose you will cross the river in our new boat, as the bridges are all burnt?

FRED STEEL.—Yes, I told Frank that I should be there to-night, and he must have everything ready for me. Gen Morgan will have a horse for me on the other side.

All exeunt R. Enter Old Marks L.

MARKS.—Alone, alone, all, all alone! Two years ago I was happy—happy as any man in East Tennessee. How is all changed! Then I was rich—now I have nothing, not even a crust of bread! Then I was happy with my family; I had honor among my fellow men! Why this change? All because I loved the Old Flag. When the cry of war arose, what was I to do? Should I see that flag under which I had lived and prospered trailed in the dust? Should I see my country ruined, and and her just laws destroyed? Nay; should I be a

willing instrument in this work of vandalism? I
saw but one course to pursue, and, though it has cost
me dear; I thank God that he has given me strength
to pursue it thus far. How fearful the cost of
loyalty! My house burned, my wife murdered, my
eldest son hung, my youngest driven away, my
daughter nowhere to be found, and myself beaten
and left for dead! But my time had not come. I
took a solemn vow of vengeance, and sixteen guerrillas have fallen before my steady aim in atonement
of my wrongs. The debt is not paid yet. I feel
that I shall see my daughter soon. I hear that she
is somewhere in this vicinity. [Crosses the stage.]
I must try and find out what that party of guerrillas
over there are planning. I dare say they are trying
to find me, or murder some Union man. [Goes and
listens.] I have been following you for three days,
and you are one less than when you started. What!
Fred Steel a guerrilla? 'Twas you, then, who led
the gang that murdered my wife and child. You
who told me that you should never aid the Southern cause. Villain! you, too, shall die the death of
a coward and traitor; but not yet. My revenge is
sure. Ha! he comes this way. I must conceal
myself. [Hides.]

Enter Fred Steel and two Guerrillas R., and go out at L. As
soon as they pass off the stage, enter Walter Greenwood in
disguise as a guerrilla. Mr. Marks sees him, and
rises to shoot, but Greenwood makes motions to him not
to. Advances to Marks, and takes off his whiskers and
hair.

MR. MARKS.—What, Walter Greenwood?

WALTER G.—Yes, I am here. I have been here two

or three weeks hunting for you, and I hardly know how I happened to see you now. We must talk fast, as the gang have camped near here, and may see us.

MARKS.—Can you tell me where my children are?

WALTER G.—Yes; William is in the Army of the Potomac, in the same regiment with me. Alice is with Widow Powers, at the foot of the mountain, where she was put by Fred Steel as a prisoner; but Mrs. Powers is as kind to her as a mother. Steel has gone there to-night to see her, and, if possible, take her with him to Richmond.

MARKS.—Take her to Richmond?

WALTER G.—Yes, Steel has received a commission as Colonel. He has been assigned to Libby prison as commander, and starts to-night for Richmond.

MARKS.—I must go at once to my daughter, and save her from this murderer's hands, if possible.

WALTER G.—You need not fear of her going with him. Tell Alice I will see her to-morrow; but I must go back to Camp now, or they will miss me.

MARKS.—When shall you return to your regiment?

WALTER G.—In two or three days. I have got to visit the Rebel camp once more, and then I am off.

MARKS.—Be cautious, Greenwood, and not run too great a risk. I am going to see my daughter, and then start for the Army of the Potomac, and find my only boy. This is my last night on this mountain. But I must avenge my wife's murder. Good-by [Shaking hands]. Tell William that his father is alive and well, and will soon see him.

Exit Greenwood R.

I must at once start for Mrs. Powers, and see my

daughter, and, if possible, put an end to Fred Steel's vile career.

Goes and looks out at R.

I see their camp now, and Greenwood is talking with them. Now for my last shot on this mountain.

Takes aim and fires.

One more added to my revenge, and seventeen sneaking guerrillas gone to their long home. [Looking.] Ah! you are coming this way for me, are you? Good-by to Fred Steel's guerrillas and the Cumberland Mountains for the present.

ACT I.

SCENE SECOND.

ALICE.—Mrs. Powers: I have been thinking all this evening that I should again see my dear father; but I have feared that he would be murdered by Fred Steel's gang of outlaws. It is nearly midnight, and I must retire. I can not sleep lately. I can't help thinking of that dreadful night when—

MRS. POWERS.—Alice, dear, don't talk about that to-night, for you know it always makes you sick; but you are getting stronger now, and must try and persuade yourself that it was God's will, and all for the best. I know it was terrible and wicked on the part of Fred Steel to take such a bloody course, but it is done and can not now be helped. Alice, I think you will again see your father and brother.

ALICE.—It is my constant prayer that I may; but father has such bitter enemies that I believe if he were to come here to-night, and the Guerrillas should know it, they would kill him before my eyes; but not until they had passed over my dead body.

MRS. POWERS.—Come, come, Alice, don't talk any more to-night; you are tired, and I am afraid you will get excited.

ALICE.—I know it, kind friend, but I can't help it. To think that Fred Steel, that detestable coward, should act such a part—and then imprison me here, as he supposed; but thank God, I could not have fallen into kinder hands; and then to come here and talk to me of love. If I dared do it, I would send his soul before his Maker. What if Fred Steel should find out that you were a strong Union woman and all of your family loyal, and that you were helping Union prisoners across the lines almost every day, and that this house was pointed out to escaped prisoners from nearly all the Southern prisons?

MRS. POWERS,—Alice, please be more careful; you must remember not to speak of that again aloud. With God's help we will keep it a secret, and as long as I have a crust of bread in the house, just so long shall I be happy to give it to the Boys in Blue.

MARY.—Come, Alice, we will now retire and get some rest; you know we can not tell what the morrow will bring forth. I dare say Fred Steel will be here to look after your welfare, and see that you do not escape. I wonder where Sam is? he has not gone to bed yet; you know we sent him out about 8 o'clock to see if there were any escaped prisoners to help, and he has not yet returned.

ALICE.—I don't know, Mary. I have been thinking of that myself, and can not tell what has———

Enter Sam, cautiously, at L. conducting an escaped Union prisoner.

SAM.—Missus, dis yer poor sojer boy is starved most to death, but he is feard you is Sesesh and gwine to send him back to Castle Thunder or Castle Lightning, or some other drefful place. I tole him don't be feard. But, Missus Powers, you must be careful for I 'spec Fred Steel is coming. [Exit L.]

MRS. POWERS.—My dear boy where have you come from ? You need not be afraid to tell, for we are all your friends.

ROBERT DAVIS.—Two weeks ago three of us got out of Salisbury prison. The other two boys were caught and killed in my sight. I had climbed a tree just soon enough to save my life. The Rebels tried to make them tell where I was; but they would not, and died with the secret in their breasts. I have traveled by night, sleeping where I could find a shelter, or lying out, with my eyes turned toward the bright stars, and dropping asleep wondering if people there suffered so. I have had very little to eat, and am sick and tired. I only ask that I may again be well enough to get back to my regiment.

MRS. POWERS.—Cheer up, my brave boy ; you at last have found friends. Here you are safe. We will soon find a way to help you to freedom and safety.

ROBERT DAVIS.—How your kind words cheer me. They are so different from what I have heard for the last six months. I feel new life and strength.

Loud raps heard at the door.

MRS. P.—Mary, show this soldier where to conceal himself, and then see who is at the door.

Mary goes L. and points out. Exit Robert Davis. Loud raps continued at the door. Mary takes the candle, and opens the door, when Fred Steel enters.

FRED STEEL.—Good evening, ladies; I am quite late.

MARY.—What brings you here at this time of night?

FRED STEEL.—I have received a commission as Colonel for my brave deeds on these mountains, and have been ordered to Richmond to take charge of the Yankee boarding house—what is better known as Libby Prison. And as I had a little time, I thought I would come and see my dear Alice before I left, hoping she would like to go to Richmond with me as Mrs. Col. Steel.

ALICE.—NEVER!

FRED STEEL.—Mrs. Powers, you and Mary can retire. I will keep guard over Alice until I call you.

Mrs. Powers and Mary retire L.

F. S.—[Advancing toward Alice] Alice, my dear, why look so scornful? Be cheerful—come, come now, don't act so. You know I love you. [Takes hold of her arm.]

ALICE.—[Striking his hand away] Unhand me, sir; your fingers are stained with my mother's blood.

FRED STEEL.—Alice, don't speak of that again—let it pass: you know I never intended to shoot your mother.

ALICE.—Why do you come to taunt me with your tales of love? You who murdered my mother and brother, and tried to murder my father.

FRED STEEL.—Alice I have often asked your forgiveness for the deeds of that dreadful night.

ALICE.—Fred Steel, I wish to ask you one question, and I want an honest answer. Why did you take such a cowardly part in this wicked Rebellion, going from house to house in the dead of night and murdering defenceless people? Old men and women, and even innocent children, have died at the hands of your fiendish gang.

FRED STEEL.—Why ask me such questions? Did I not rid the country of nearly all the Yankee spies in this section. I would not harm a woman or a child, if they did not interfere with my business. Furthermore, I was promised a commission if I made way with these traitors. Honestly, Alice, I have often wished I had not taken the course I have; but it is now too late.

ALICE.—No, not too late; burn your Rebel commission; go North; put on a blue coat, and help crush the greatest and most wicked rebellion the world ever saw.

FRED STEEL.—What! give up a Colonel's commission, and be a private soldier?

ALICE.—Yes; and be a man.

FRED STEEL.—Never! I yet will hold a commission still higher then Colonel. But I must not stop to talk with you; I am going to start for Richmond at once, and you are going with me. So make haste.

ALICE.—Fred Steel, I am not going with you.

FRED STEEL.—It will be useless to resist, as I have a guard at the door, to help me if necessary.

ALICE.—For shame, Fred Steel! Had you the whole Confederate army at your command I would not go.

FRED STEEL.—[Advancing and seizing Alice by the arms.] Miss Marks, you are in my power, and I will make you my wife, by fair means or foul.

Mr. Marks enters cautiously from L., and seizes Steel, and sends him to R.

ALICE.—[Rushing forward and embracing her father.] Father! Father!

MARKS.—Villain! we have met at last, face to face, and now for my revenge.

FRED STEEL.—Old man, I have come to make a wife of that girl, and am going to do it; if you interfere you are a dead man. [Whistles.]

Enter two guerrillas from R. and seize Mr. Marks.

Bind him fast, boys, and take him to camp. Do what you please with him.

MARKS.—Fred Steel, I am on your track. You are doomed to die the death of a miserable, sneaking traitor.

FRED STEEL.—[Pointing his revolver at Marks.] Silence, you old fool, or I'll put a hole through you.

ALICE.—[Stepping in between Steel and her father.] Shoot! shoot! if you dare, you villain. You are a coward; you dare not shoot. Stained with blood as your hands are, you dare not murder me. Injure one hair of my father's head, and you will not go from this house alive.

FRED STEEL.—Not quite so smart. You can't scare anybody. [Advances.] Come, hurry up, the guard at the boat will think we are never coming. [Advances and seizes Alice.] Come, boys, take the old man along.

ALICE.—Help! help! I can not, I will not go! Unhand me, villain.

Enter Robert Davis and Sam at L. who at once seize the guard holding Mr. Marks, disarm and drive them off the stage— Re-enter Sam, who points revolver at Fred Steel—Steel releases Alice.

ALICE.—Not yet, Sam, he is not fit to die. (Pointing to Fred Steel.) Go, sir, your presence is loathsome.

Exit Sam at L.

FRED. S.—Who is this nigger and that escaped prisoner?

ALICE.—Go, sir, and ask no questions.

FRED S.—(Retiring slowly.) Young lady you will be fearfully sorry for this gross insult. You have defeated me this time. I shall leave my Company in trusty hands, and they will deal with you as you deserve. As for your old father there, he *can not* escape my vengeance—he must and *shall* yield to the will of Fred Steel's Rangers. He can not cross the river now, the bridges are all burned, and there is but one boat, and that *we* use, and no one else. I have a trusty man in charge of it, so I will bid you good-by. My revenge is sure.

Exit Fred Steel R.

MARKS.—Gone—and Old Marks' curses follow you.

ALICE.—Dear father, what shall we do? I do not fear Fred Steel, or his gang, but I do feel so lonesome without you are with me. Let us go to Knoxville. Mrs. Powers wishes to go at once, and we shall be so happy there. No fear of Guerrillas.

MARKS.—No, daughter, I can not go to Knoxville. I am going North, to find William. We can see each other but a short time, for I must start to-night.

ALICE.—I can not say "no," although it is hard to part with you so soon.

MARKS.—Yes, I must go this very night; but how can I cross the river?

ALICE.—I will get a canteen of whisky and drug it. We will send Sam ahead, and he can get the guard drunk who has charge of their boat. Then you can cross the river, and very soon find friends, for you know just what house to go to for help over there. We will go at once and prepare for your departure.

MARKS.—Where is Sam? We must see him and make arrangements at once, for I am going to take him with me. "Sam!" "Samuel!"

Enter Sam at L.

SAM.—Yes, Massa, I's here. Whar is de big Steel, am he done gone?

MARKS.—Yes, Sam, Steel has gone, and you and I are going North to-night. We will go and see William and the soldiers. Don't you want to go?

SAM.—Yes, Massa, I wants to go; but who will take keer of Miss Alice?

ALICE.—I am going to Knoxville to-morrow with Mrs. Powers, to stay until father gets back. We have made all the arrangements. You and the sol-dier are to go first and get the boat at the river, and then father will come. He will go down the river about a mile, and take you and the soldier on board, and convey you to a place of safety.

Sam.—I's gwine for to be a soldier. I's gwine to be a Colored Regiment, and have a brass coat wid blue buttons all over it. I guess Mr. Lincum will be glad when he hears I's coming. I golly what would hab become of dis country if dis yah niggah never had no mammy ?

Exit L.

Marks.—Come, Alice, I must be going, Sam will be ready in a few minutes.

Exit all at L.

ACT I.

SCENE THIRD.

Wood Scene—Enter Sam and Robert Davis at L.

ROBERT DAVIS.—Come, Sam, hurry up; We shan't get there to-night, unless we go faster.

SAM.—I's hurryin' fast I can. You see, Massa, I don't want to found any dem Guerillas, cause we haint got no time to stop and kill 'em.

Lightning flashes and thunder heard, which very much frightens Sam.

Who's feard? Guess I ain't; dat's thunder and lightning. You ain't skeered, is you?

ROBERT DAVIS.—What ails you, Sam, hurry up, we shall get wet if we don't look out? It is going to rain, and I am afraid we won't get to the boat and get that whisky into the guard before Mr. Marks comes. [Exit both at R.]

Enter Marks and Alice L.—Lightning and thunder at intervals.

ALICE.—This is a dreadful night, father; but I am happy to think you are to be safe soon.

MARKS.—Yes, I rejoice to think that I shall soon breathe the air of freedom. Sam is a trusty boy, and I have no fear from him.

ALICE.—I have no fear from him; but I am fearful that we have been watched by the Guerrillas. Hist! I can hear them now. Oh! let us hurry. [Exit both at R.]

Enter Guerrillas at L.

SAM SMITH.—I am sure I saw Old Marks and Alice come out of the house, and come this way. We must have Old Marks this very night, and that nigger, too. Steel trusted that black devil too much. I just want to get hold of his carcass. I'll fix him. See! [All look out at R.] There goes Old Marks and Alice! They are going for our boat. Look down to the river. That nigger has unloosed the boat! Where is the Guard? They must have killed him. Come on, boys. [All exit at R.]

Shouts heard outside of "Shoot him," Shoot the gal, and the Nigger, if you can't take them alive"—One shot heard Alice enters at 1st R. E., kneels, clasps hands, exclaims : "Saved ! Saved ! "—Scene rises showing Mr. Marks in boat crossing river—He fires one shot and shouts, "Old Marks is safe !"—Back scene rises showing Goddess of Liberty.

ACT II.

SCENE FIRST.

W ALTER G.—Corporal, I guess you had better take the men and go out a little nearer the Rebel line, and should you see or hear anything that would lead you to think they intend to give us battle, report the same to me at once.

PAT.—Yis, Corporal, fall in your min to onst, and Pat O'Doherty will bring up the rare. I will be on the lookout that none ov um lag behind, and as sure as a Johnny spakes a loud word, I'll be afther reportin' to Capt. Grainwood.

CORPORAL.—Fall in, men.

Men all fall in except Greenwood, Mr. Marks and Wm. Marks.

SAM H.—De Lord bress my soul, Massa Greenwood, is you gwine to hab a battle here ?

W ALTER G.—It looks so now, Sam ; but I thought you were anxious to see us pitch into the Rebels?

SAM.—Yes, Massa, an so I is ; but can't I wait till de sun shines, it would be mighty dark seein' you shoot now?

PAT.—Sam Hannibal, yes kin come along wid me, an I don't think ye nade be throubled wid fare while under me spishal protecshin.

SAM.—Yah, yah; dis yer chile aint afeard to go wid you; you's a man after my own heart, and if de Rebble sojers come when we git dah, I guess day will be sorry.

WALTER G.—Yes, Sam, you go with Pat. I shall not need you here. Now don't run or get frightened, but keep close to Pat.

Corporal drills his squad a little, and marches them off at R

MARKS.—Well, boys, here I am, free from the hands of Fred Steel's band, and where I feel that I can strike one more blow at the heart of treason.

WILLIAM.—Yes, father, I am happy to see you and have you so near me; but you are too old to try to march with us day by day, and suffer the exposure of a soldier's life.

MARKS.—My dear boy, you little know what privations are. I have lived through two years of camp life such as would make you faint hearted. No, no, my boy, don't think that of me until you see me lag behind on the march.

WALTER G.—I guess you hadn't better try to talk camp life with your father, for he can tell you more about it than you know yourself.

WILLIAM.—I know he has had a hard time, and that is just the reason why I think he needs rest. But if he feels it his duty to go as a soldier, I have nothing more to say.

MARKS.—Just as long as Fred Steel's band of Guerrillas exist, just so long will Old Marks be on their trail—be it in the Army of the Potomac or on the mountains of East Tennessee. I feel that a blow here will do just as much good as to shoot one of his gang.

Walter G.—Wherever a blow is struck at treason, it is felt the whole length of the line. But, Mr. Marks, you are not free from Guerrillas here. Our regiment has been harrassed by Mosby's gang for more than three weeks, and I fear more from them to-night than from the Rebel troops. Our Regiment sleep on their arms night after night to be in readiness for just such an attack. I gave the Corporal strict orders to keep a sharp lookout at the outer picket post, and if he should see any Guerrillas or anything that would lead him to think there was to be an attack by Rebel troops or Guerrillas, to send a man here at once.

William.—Don't you think, Walter, that we had better try and get a little rest? We were up all last night, and have had but little sleep to-day.

Walter G.—I have been thinking of that myself, for I know we have a trusty guard at the outer post, and we should be warned soon enough were we all asleep.

Marks.—Hark! I thought I heard the pickets firing. There goes another shot. Our boys are having a skirmish.

Walter G.—If there is any trouble, we shall hear of it soon, for the Corporal will either send a man or come himself.

Enter Pat O'Doherty and Sam Hannibal all out of breath.

Pat.—Faith, an' yer honor, Captain, an', an', the guerrillas is afther us, the whole of Mosby's army. And the Corporal towld me to be afther comin' here and tellin' yes at onst, and, by the howly Moses, sich a time as I have had a gettin' here. In the fust place, I made a mistake and run the wrong way intirely; then I got twisted about and run the other way; thin I wint back and axed the Corporal what he wanted I should bring him, when he sint me away, and towld me to tell the Captain that Mosby was fightin' him, and that you must sind a man to camp to onst and tell the Colonel that there was trouble on the picket line, and tor the Colonel to send word to the Gineral, and the Gineral tell the min to be ready to fight. And now, Captain, I want to be the man to go and tell the Colonel, for I know all about it. [Spatting his hand.] Be out of that, you skater, and would you be afther sucking the blood of Pat O'Doherty, when he is on important business? Now for the Colonel's tent. [Exit Pat at L. in haste.

SAM.—Captain, dis niggah gwine to keep close to Pat. [Exit at L.]

Three shots heard at R—Union pickets back on the stage from R closely followed by guerrillas—Walter Greenwood and Mr. Marks taken prisoners—Union troops driven back off stage L—Guerrillas commence robbing the dead and wounded—Guerrillas make remarks about what they find, &c—Volley musketry heard at L—Some of the guerrillas fall—The rest retreat off at R—Enter Union regiment at charge bayonets.

ACT II.

SCENE SECOND.

Same as Scene I, Act 2d—Curtain rises—No one to be seen—
Soon Sam cautiously makes his appearance at L loudly calling for Patrick O'Doherty, advances to center of stage and
stops.

SAM.—I aren't feard to be here alone, but Massa
Greenwood tole me to keep with Patrick; but de
Lor bress my soul, I couldn't no more keep np wid
him than I could cotch chain lightning by de tail.
He's a drefful runnist. Jes so soon as he tole Massa
Greenwood dat de Guerillas was a comin, he run fer
de Kernul's tent, and tole him, and I tried mighty
hard to keep wid him, but wan't runnist nuff to keep
nigh him, and fore day got fru fightin' I lost sight
ob him, and now whar is he? De Guerillas haint
got him prisoner, kase he didn't run in dat direction.
He mus be round here somewhar. Massa Greenwood tole me to keep clos to Patrick O'Doherty
until he wanted me, and now I mus found him.
(Loudly calling) Patrich O———'Doherty, Pos'
No. 15th amendment, double quick, march.

Enter Pat at R slowly, with coat very badly torn, and otherwise
generally demoralized, but does not see Sam at first.

PAT.—Am I Patrick O'Dohirety entirely, or am I
his ghost? Strange that the boys should run and
lave me alone. What the divil do they think to run
and lave me to fight the whole Guerrilla army? and
Samuel Hannibal, too, he was scart and run, and

even after Capum Grainwood towld him to keep clost
to me. Just a minute ago I thought I heard Patrick
O'Doherty's name mintioned. I wonder what it
could mane? I must look around a little and see if
I can find any of the boys. I am not at all frightened, and can whip all the Ribels in a batch, if they
will only come on.

Goes and looks out at L, when he hears a dog bark or a
   pig squeal, which frightens him, and he leaps back on the
   stage—All this time Sam is very much pleased to see the
   fun go on, but does not make a loud noise

It must be a bloody Guerrilla, and I must be afther
getting out of this intirely, or I shall be down to
Libby prison before I want to go.

He turns and starts to run, but is so near Sam that he hits him
   hard enough to knock both down.

PAT.—Why the divil didn't ye tell me that ye
wanted me to ground arms, and not be afther execut-
ing yer orders until after yer had given 'em.

SAM.—Lor' bress my soul, Pat, how easy we did
parade rest.

PAT.—Divil a bit ov rest did I git, but plenty of
parade.

SAM.—Patrick, what made you run off and leave
me when Massa Greenwood tole you to stay wid me?

PAT.—Capum Grainwood didn't tell me to stay
wid you. He told you to stay wid me. Now why
didn't you obey orders? If yes keep on disobeying
orders in that way, Capum Grainwood will be after
rejucing you to the ranks of a private, and then yes
will have to obey orders. But come, Samuel, we

must find the Regiment. I don't see how I come to get astray.

SAM.—Patrick, Massa Greenwood and Massa Marks are both prisoners. I helped Massa William to get away, but I could not help de other two. I was feared de Guerrillas would come back; but I 'spect day am done gone. Massa William feels drefful bad because his fader am taken prisoner.

Enter three Guerrillas, who chase Sam and Pat around the stage —Curtain drops.

ACT III.

SCENE FIRST.

Libby Prison—Prisoners seated in groups on the floor closely watched by Rebel Guard.

ROBERT DAVIS.—Charley, did you see the New York Tribune, this morning, when old Ben had it?

CHARLEY BATES.—No, Robert; but I heard some of the boys say that the Rebs would exchange prisoners before long. If we can tell anything by the papers, Grant is at Vicksburg, and is bound to stay there, until he either takes it or dies in the attempt.

ROBERT D.—I only hope he will succeed. I have have been in Salisbury prison, and I think I know what the horrors of a Rebel prison are; but I would willingly stay here a month longer if I could only hear that Vicksburg had fallen.

JOHN STEEL.—Robert, I wish I could be as cheerful as you are. But here I have been for a long time; at first I was cheerful, and tried to have courage; but as the news of victory after victory for the Union army come to the ears of the Rebels, the harder they have been upon us, until nearly all that came here with me have starved to death, or been shot for some slight offence.

REBEL GUARD, GEO. MACK.—(Striking John), Shut up yer head, you detestable Yankee, yer no need ter come ter war if yer hadn't wanted ter.

John S.—I know that, sir; but I would not stay away when such as you were engaged in trying to destroy the liberty our grandfathers fought for. I have but a short time to live, but with my dying breath will I rejoice that I have remained true to my dear dead mother's last request of loyalty to the glorious old flag.

Marks.—Brave boy; should you live to get out of this hell hole, you will be proud to say that, tempted by the devil as you were, loyalty triumphed, while *he* (pointing to Rebel Guard) taints the very earth with treason, and to his dying day can not forget that he has been a traitor to the old flag.

Walter Greenwood.—Boys, keep up good courage. We shall not stop here long, starved and abused as we are. These wretches can not keep us here always. There is a good time coming, and that soon.

Reb. Geo. M.—Yes, you-uns talk well, don't yer? but I reckon you-uns will have some o' yer pluck taken out of yer 'fore night, for we-un's new commander has come, and he won't stand none of yer Yankee slang. He's a goin' through the boardin' house purty quick, and I rackon most of you-uns will sing a different song when you see him.

Enter Fred Steel.

Fred Steel.—Hello, Yanks! I reckon you are all glad to see me, and I suppose the Sergeant told you I was coming. Now I want you all to behave yourselves, and I won't hurt you; but if you don't mind you will be sorry. I shall not have any candles burned in the night, as you might burn us all up, nor shall I have any reading going on, for I want you to keep thinking of your guilty crimes and what you are here for. [Looking to the Rebel Guards.] Now, Guards, do your duty like men, and if you see any of the Yanks disobey orders, either shoot 'em or let me know of it, and I will take care of them. [Looking to John Steel.] Here, you villain, what are you doing? Didn't I just give orders not to have any reading go on? Give me that book.

JOHN. S.—Please let me keep it; it won't do me any harm. It is the last gift of my dear mother who is dead. It is a Bible, sir, and I am sure there can be no harm in my reading it.

FRED S.—Give me that book, you mudsill.

JOHN S.—Please let me keep it. I will not read it any more. I will keep it in my bosom, and no one shall see it. It has my name written it by dear dead mother. She wrote it just as I started for the war, and told me always to keep it. So please don't take it away. I can not give it up.

Fred Steel knocks John down, takes the Bible, and throws it away.

FRED S.—There, Yanks, now see if you can obey orders.

Steel now starts to go out, when he meets an old negro who has a paper sticking out of his pocket. Steel grabs it and looks at the title, and exclaims : "New York Tribune."

FRED STEEL.—You old nigger, why didn't you give me that paper when I gave orders not to have any reading going on?

OLD BEN.—Bekase, Massa, you did not ask me for it. If you had, I should surely hab gib it to you.

FRED STEEL.—Sergeant, bring me the whip. I'll teach this nigger to have New York Tribunes in his pocket.

Sergeant brings whip.

OLD BEN.—Massa, what would you whip me for, I hain't done nuffin, and will always obey you.

FRED STEEL.—(Striking Old Ben) Shut up, you old nigger, while I have charge here I am going to have order. Down on your knees, and I will take a little of the impudence out of you.

OLD BEN.—(Kneeling) Don't whip me, massa, don't. If you want to kill me, I won't say a word. But I can't be whipped any more. I have great scars all over me where I have been whipped for nuffin. Now don't whip me again.

FRED S.—Guards take the old nigger and strip him. I said I would thrash him, and I will.

Two Guards take off Ben's coat, and hold him down, when Fred Steel commences whipping him—Old Ben groans and pleads all to no purpose—He then stops groaning, moans, and is then quiet—Steel then appears to strike Ben in the head with the butt of the whip—Music : "Poor Old Slave."

WALTER G.—Fred Steel, you murderer, I will not see you pound that dead man any more. If you had any shame in you, you never would have committed such a horrid deed.

FRED S.—Who speaks my name? What! Walter Greenwood?

WALTER G.—Yes, Walter Greenwood speaks your vile name.

FRED S.—I am glad to find you here. It was only a few weeks ago that I bid farewell to your friends in East Tennessee. And I told them should you happen here, I would use the greatest care that you do not trouble the Southern cause any more. So prepare yourself (drawing a revolver), for I am going to blow your brains out.

WALTER G.—Fred Steel, I thank God I am prepared to meet my Maker ; but you are not the agent that will send my soul into eternity.

FRED S.—[Raising his revolver and taking aim.] What, what do you say, you spy ?

WALTER G.—Fred Steel, you are a coward, and just as sure as you shoot, these starved men here will tear you in pieces. We are human, and only ask to be treated as prisoners of war. We have borne our lot patiently, and have not been abused beyond endurance until you stepped your fiendish foot in here. Before we will submit to your outrages, there is not a man here but will give his life in defense of his rights.

FRED S.—Greenwood, I acknowledge to being a little too hasty. I now announce that Walter Greenwood, the Union spy, will be shot at sunset to-morrow. Now, you Yanks, see if you can behave yourselves. I shall come and see you once every day, and I hope there won't anything happen to mar your happiness. As it is getting late, you must all retire. Guards, keep good watch to-night, and to-morrow we will see some fun.

MARKS.—Go now, you Guerrilla. You have done enough. You have murdered one more man, and added one more line to your record of infamy.

FRED S.—Old Marks? How came you here?
You thought you had got out of my power when
you stole my boat, didn't you? But fortune favors
me at every step, and if you were engaged in a just
cause, you never would have been so unfortunate.

MARKS.—I am proud to say that I am fortunate,
and that you are unfortunate in having such a black
heart. I would not exchange places with you to-day.

FRED S.—One more word out of your head, and
I will blow your brains out.

MARKS.—Fred Steel, I am prepared for that. You
have done nothing else but murder for more than two
years. It would take a man a lifetime to record all
your vile acts, and do them justice.

Fred Steel draws a revolver and fires at Mr. Marks—The
ball only knocks Marks' cap off, but hits John Steel in the
neck.

JOHN S.—(Screaming and falling forward) Oh!
I'm shot! I'm shot!

MARKS.—Murderer! you are not satisfied with
murdering one man, but must take the life of your
own brother, who has been ashamed to own you.
First you take his Bible away, and, not content with
that, deliberately shoot him—and your angel
mother looking down on you. Go, sir, before
I kill you. I will tear you in pieces, if you do not
take your vile carcass out of my presence.

JOHN S.—Don't talk so. Mr. Marks. He is
my brother. He didn't mean to shoot me. Had I
told him who I was, he would have been kind to me.

'Please hold my head for me. It is getting dark, and my head is dizzy.

Mr. Marks gets behind John and holds his head on his bosom.

FRED S.—Are you my brother John? Is mother dead?

JOHN S.—Yes, I am your brother; but very soon you will be alone. My strength is fast failing. Dear mother is dead. She died soon after we reached Boston. I enlisted at once on arriving in Boston, and soon after coming to the front I heard of her death. Her last request to you was to remain true to the old flag.

FRED S.—It is too late now. I am a Colonel in the Confederate army, and if you had told me who you were when I first came in, I should have taken you out of here at once. I didn't mean to shoot you. I am sorry I did.

JOHN S.—Don't feel bad, brother. I shall soon be better off. It was only an act of kind Providence to relieve me from my tortures. I should have lived but a few days. I will tell mother that you did not mean to shoot me, and that you are sorry. Come nearer, brother, I can not see you, it is so dark. Hark! oh, such sweet music. It is growing lighter now; mother is coming to see us; we are at home now, brother; no more war. Come, mother, and let me kiss you. Sister Clara what makes you look so sad? mother is happy, and wants me to come to her. I am coming, mother.

Prisoners all point fingers in scorn at Fred Steel, who stands at R. of stage with folded arms—Back scene rises showing angel with arms outstretched toward John Steel.

ACT III.

SCENE SECOND.

Outside of Libby Prison—Rebels doing guard duty.

ABRAHAM ALLEN.—I'll be darned if I ain't ashamed of doing this kind of business. I'd rather be one of them fellers in there than to be prowlin' 'round here with orders to shoot one on um if I see him a lookin' outen the winder. I tried to go North when the war broke out, but I wan't smart, and got picked up at it, and was forced into this colored wardrobe; but I don't think I have done um much good. I know one thing, I never hurt a Union soldier yet, and I never will. But the first chance I get I will cross the line and join the Union army— and then I can go into battle feelin' that there is something to fight for; and, with the old Stars and Stripes floatin' overhead, I can whip the whole Southern Confederacy and stand Jeff Davis on his ear. Hurrah! Hurrah for the flag of the free. [Guard sees Corporal of the Guard coming.] Shut up there, you cussed Yanks, or I will give you a dose of lead that I stole away from one of you.

CORPORAL.—What is all this fuss about?

ABRAHAM A.—O, them Yanks are having a sort of Fourth of July, and I am just going to stop it.

CORPORAL.—That is right, make a hole through the first one you can get a chance at.

A. A.—Don't I, Corporal, don't I shoot at um most every night? Say, Corporal, can't you get me a furlough?

CORPORAL.—I don't know, I will see next month; I can tell better after I see how many Yanks you shoot.

Exit Corporal.

A. A.—Well, if that is my only chance, I don't see but what I am in for the war, unless sooner deserted. I don't like this. If I could only throw open that prison door and free all them poor boys, it would be the happiest time of my life; but I can't, and 'tain't no use a whinin'. Hello! who in thunder is that? Oh, it's Aunt Nancy with some more things for the poor soldiers.

Enter woman closely veiled, with a basket of crackers, &c.— Guard takes it and passes the contents into the prison, giving the basket back to the woman, who goes out—Guard resumes his beat—Officer of the day passes, giving orders to keep strict watch.

A. A.—(Looking at his watch) It is almost one o'clock, and I shall soon be relieved. They always put me on this post, cause they know I'm faithful.

Union prisoners begin to put their heads up out of the ground look around, dodge back, and finally one crawls out and creeps off on his hands and knees, when the Guard crys out: "Post No. 7, one o'clock, and all is well"— More prisoners come up out of the ground and run off— After they have all come up, the relief comes around and relieves the Guard—As they pass off they discover the tunnel, and at once give the alarm, when all is confusion— Curtain.

ACT IV.

SCENE FIRST.

Woods—Guerrilla camp—Walter Greenwood disguised as Joe Blake, a Guerrilla.

FRED STEEL.—Well, boys, I am glad to be with you again. I did not like Libby at all, and resigned my position there to return to these mountains once more.

TOM JONES.—And we are glad to see you back. We have had dull times since you were here. We have had hard work to get our rations most of the time.

SAM SMITH.—Yes, Colonel, that's so; we havn't spotted any of them Yanks for more'n a week, and when you was here we got plenty of chances at 'em. Tell you what it is, Colonel, we ain't always poked 'em over when we oughter; but somehow most of us hain't got the pluck, unless they get us mad.

TOM JONES.—We have been thinking of giving up this company and dividing up into gangs of five or six, and try it that way; but just as we would get ready to try it on, we would run on to a squad of Yanks, and it would take us all to fight 'em—and so we have kept together and kept fightin' until more than half of our original men are dead.

SAM S.—I tell yer what 'tis, Colonel, we made money when we was up by Cumberland Gap, but after you went away the Yanks soon drove us out, and they have kept us on the move most of the time since. But we have got lots of horses since you have been away.

FRED S.—I am sorry to hear that so many of my brave boys are dead; but such is the fortune of war, and we all must take our chances. I see some faces here that I never saw before, but dare say they are all right, and ready to fight for our black flag and strike a blow for Southern homes.

SAM S.—You see, Colonel, we was all so glad to see you back that we forgot to say anything to you about it. Here is Joe Blake, just come from the Yankee army. He tells us that there will be hot work here soon, and that we shall have plenty to do.

FRED S.—I knew that the Yanks were after us before, and they are bound to follow us until they shoot us all, so we must be on watch for them.

JOE BLAKE.—I only left Burnside's army last week, and I tell you you have got to be sharp or they will go for you.

SAM S.—By the way, Colonel, what ever became of that gal you used to think so much of and was going to marry?

FRED S.—She is in Knoxville now, and we must plan some way to get hold of her before Burnside gets there, for old man Marks, his son, and that villain, Greenwood, are all with Burnside, and of course when they get to Knoxville they will find her and send her North, and that will be the last of her, so far as I am concerned.

Tom J.—Where is your mother now, Colonel, didn't she go to Knoxville?

Fred S.—Yes, she was there, but just before the war commenced she and my brother John went to Boston. She died there. She was full of Yankee patriotism, and had a good deal to say about the old flag, the land our fathers fought for, and all that sort of stuff. John was just like her, and always said that if there was a war he should go North and enlist. He did so, and died in Libby prison. My sister Clara, I suppose, is still in Knoxville, although I have not heard from her for more than a year.

Joe B.—What about that gal? Get that fixed up some way Maybe we can have a little fun out of it. Sam told me all about the old man, Marks, so I know what you want. If we can only plan to get hold of her.

Fred S.—I'll tell you, boys, what I think I'll do: I will disguise myself and go to Knoxville and find out all I can. Then we shall know just what to do.

Sam S.—No, Colonel, I don't think that will answer, for we are so near Knoxville that I am afraid they will mistrust you, and we shall all be gobbled up. You would have to be there two or three days. We must do something else that won't take up so much time, for old Burnside is north of Loudon now, and that is only a few miles from Knoxville.

Joe B.—I have it. We will write the gal a letter, and sign Walter Greenwood's name to it. · You see she knows that he is with Burnside, and she will think it is all right.

Fred S.—What will you write?

Joe B.—Why most anything that will bring her
out of Knoxville. [Writing.] Let me see. [Reads
aloud.] "*Miss Alice Marks:* Burnside will be in
Knoxville next week. Meet me on Saturday in
the woods just north of the four corners on the
road that leads from Knoxville to Strawberry Plains.
You may think this a strange request, but you can
be of great service to the Northern troops, and I
know you will esteem it a privilege to help them.
Meet me at sunset. There is a loyal family near by
with whom I have made arrangements for you to
stop over night. Come alone, as we do not know
whom to trust, and if you take anyone with you we
may have trouble. Your friend and protector—W.
Greenwood." There, I reckon that will be sweet
enough.

Fred S.—Good! I never should have thought of
such a plan. I wish you had been with us from the
first; we should not have slipped up on so many of
our plans. Now, Sam, will you take the job of giving that letter to Miss Alice? You will only have
to find where Mrs. Powers lives, and then you will
find Alice. Give her the letter, and come away before she has a chance to read it, as she may wish to
ask you questions.

Sam S.—Yes, Colonel; just the job I want, and I
think the letter will bring her. I'll be back before
morning, and I suppose that on Sunday we shall have
a wedding.

Exit Sam Smith at R.

Fred S.—Now, boys, I want four or five of you
to go up to Strawberry Plains and see how things

look. Be sure and return as soon as Saturday noon, as we may want you Saturday night. Tom, you had better sort of look out for things, as you know the country so well. We must all meet here again on Saturday.

Exit all at L.

ACT IV.

SCENE SECOND.

Mrs. Powers' home in Knoxville—Mary Powers reading a paper
—Mrs. Powers and Alice variously employed.

MARY.—How dreadful it is to read of the sacrifice
of so many lives, the destruction of so much prop-
erty, and the desolation of our country by civil war.
When will it end? When will the South return to
its allegiance?

MRS. POWERS.—Mary, we have much to be thankful for. Our little home has been laid waste, but our
lives have been spared, and we have found dear
friends here. The war must close soon. The South
can hold out but a little longer, and then we will return to our home and see what we can do toward
repairing the waste of war. I fervently hope, too,
that Alice may have her father and brother restored
in safety to her.

ALICE.—Yes, my dear friends, it is my constant
prayer that my dear father and brother return alive.
Oh, what anguish I have suffered during this dreadful
war. But I am thankful that my lot is no worse.
How many loyal mountaineers of East Tennessee
have gone to their long home. Still they were firm,
and even to-day there are men on the mountains who
are anxiously awaiting Burnside's arrival to strike
a blow for loyalty.

MRS. P.—Thank God the time has about come,
for Burnside will soon be here. O, how many pray-

ers of thanksgiving will go up to heaven when the fife and drum of the Northern army, shall be heard in Knoxville. How many poor souls will be ready to worship almost the soldiers who set them free from this little else than prison.

ALICE.—History will never record the many, very many valuable lives sacrificed in our State. There is no section of the country where there have been such mean, contemptible, bloodthirsty schemes resorted to as have here been practiced by the Guerrillas. They are not subject even to the lax military rule of the so-called Confederacy, and so they execute their wicked deeds without hindrance or fear of punishment, murdering little children, women, aged men, in fact every one unfortunate enough to fall into their hands.

MRS. P.—When the Union army comes there will be a different order of things. It will be a happy moment when the loyal veterans march through our streets, the bands playing the tunes we used to hear, and the old flag floating over all. What a load will be lifted from the true hearts of Tennessee when that time comes. Let us have a song.

Mary Powers sings the "Star Spangled Banner."

MRS. P.—Yes, long may it wave. Those words never seemed so dear to me as they have since the dark days of this terrible war.

Raps heard at the door—Alice goes and opens it and Clara Steel enters.

ALICE.—Dear Clara, I wish you had been here just now. Mary has been singing that dear old song,

"The Star Spangled Banner," and I believe it never sounded so sweet to me as now.

CLARA.—It is a soul-inspiring tune. How I long to hear it played again by some martial band.

MARY.—You will not have long to wait, for we have heard, very reliably, that the Northern troops will be here within a week.

CLARA.—Happy shall I be to see them. But Fred, alas! will not be with them. Oh! if I could only see him long enough to tell him of mother's dying request, he could not continue in his present wicked work. I fear he is dead. The last I knew ot him was through the papers, that he was in command of Libby prison. Then I read that he had gone from there. Where is he now?

ALICE.—You may yet see him. I do not think he is dead. He is your brother, I know, and as such you love him, and would be happy to see him give up his wicked course.

Raps heard at door—Mary goes and opens it—Enter Guerrilla.

SAM SMITH.—Is Miss Alice Marks in?

ALICE.—Yes, sir, that is my name; what do you wish?

SAM S.—(Handing her a letter) Here is a letter I was requested to deliver to you, and to no one else. It is a private affair, I believe. [Exit.]

Alice opens the letter and reads it to herself several times. then looks around the room as if to see if anyone is listening, when she reads it aloud.

"*Miss Alice Marks:* Burnside will be in Knoxville next week. Meet me on Saturday in the woods just north of the four corners on the road that leads from

Knoxville to Strawberry Plains. You may think this a strange request, but you can be of great service to the Northern troops, and I know you will esteem it a privilege to help them. Meet me at sunset. There is a loyal family near by with whom I have made arrangements for you to stop over night. Come alone, as we do not know whom to trust, and if you take anyone with you we may have trouble. Your friend and protector—W. GREENWOOD." (Laying the letter down.) What can that mean? What can he want of me? Why it is nearly five miles there, and he wants me to come to-night. It is very strange. Where is the man who brought the letter? Mrs. Powers, what shall I do?

MRS. P.—It is very strange. I don't see why he didn't come himself. Let me see the letter. [Takes the letter.] It looks like Mr. Greenwood's writing. I should almost be afraid to go, but still if you can be of any service to the Union troops you should surely go.

ALICE.—But he wants me to go alone.

CLARA.—You must not go alone. I will go with you. We will each take a pistol for use in case of need. I can conceal myself near you, and be ready to help in case you need assistance.

ALICE.—I wish you would go with me, Clara, I am afraid to go alone. It will do no harm, as Walter's caution was only given through fear of being betrayed. He is very careful, and neglects no precaution. He has always taken care of himself when he has been alone. He has been many times within the Rebel lines, and never has been detected yet.

MRS. P.—Well, girls, you must make haste. It is a long distance there, and you want to walk slow.

ALICE.—Let me get my things, and we will be off at once. I almost dread to go, the country is so full of Guerrillas; but they will not dare come so near to Knoxville. [Exit.]

ACT IV.

SCENE THIRD.

Same as Scene First, Act IV.

FRED STEEL.—(Walking back and forth) I don't see what keeps Sam so long. He said that he would be back before morning, and he has been gone three days already. I fear he has been gobbled up by some of Burnside's scamps. [Drinks.]

TOM JONES.—Don't you worry, Colonel. Sam is all right; he will be here before long, too. You see, Colonel, the Yanks are all around now, and a man has to be purty sharp, or they will nab him. Then you know there is lots and lots of these mountaineers that are Yankee clear to their backbone, though we have rid the country of some of them.

JOE BLAKE.—Yes, Tom, it is a fact. And, although we claim that we are all right, we must confess that the people around these mountains have suffered more than in any section of the country. You know we hear almost every day of their leaving the mountains to join the Northern army.

FRED S.—A man would think you were a full-blooded Yankee to hear you talk.

JOE B.—I can't help that. I can not but admire their pluck.

TOM J.—Hark! I heard some one coming.

They all take their guns as if ready for action—Enter Sam S. at L.

SAM S.—Wall, boys, did you think I'd got nabbed? Not yet ; but I did have to work purty sharp some of the time, and I don't want to go galling any more. I never found her till to-day, and I hurried right back for fear she would be here first. I don't blame you, Colonel, for wanting that gal ; but I believe I should rather get her by courtin', for she looks to me as if she would take care of No. 1, let her be where she would. I stopped at the door and listened just as long as I dared, and she read the letter to um all, and she is comin'.

JOE B.—Did you hear her say anything about the writing?

SAM S.—Yes, the women folks all looked at it, and they said it was Walter Greenwood's writing. So I concluded that he wrote letters to her, and that the Colonel's chance was purty slim.

FRED S.—Not so slim after all. If she comes here to-night we will make her a prisoner, and to-morrow I will start with her for Longstreet's camp, where I can find a chaplain without any trouble. We will be married, and then go to England. I think by that time she will be humbled enough to behave herself and treat me as a devoted husband should be treated. Here's fun. [Drinks.] Let's all take something. [Drinks.]

SAM S.—I glory in your spunk, Colonel ; but don't you think that plan is more easily made than executed ?

FRED S.—What is there to hinder carrying it out?

SAM S.—You see Burnside is up this side of Loudon, and will be in Knoxville next week ; and if you start for Longstreet's camp you may find it occupied by Burnside. If so, you won't find any chaplain to perform the ceremony.

FRED S.—Don't you worry about me. I never did slip up on any such plan yet. I don't propose to go to Burnside's camp yet awhile. Why don't you take something? [Drinks.]

TOM J.—You fellers had better stop that talk and make arrangements about meeting that gal, for I believe she will be here on time. If Sam tells the truth about her being so smart.

FRED S.—Yes, boys, we must fix that up right off, for it is almost time she was here.

SAM S.—It won't do for us all to stay here. She may see us before we see her, and then she won't come. I don't think she would like the looks of us very well.

FRED S.—That's so, and I hardly know how to arrange it. All hands had better take something. [Drinks.]

JOE B.—Some of the boys ought to be on the lookout for Yanks, for we don't know when we are safe.

FRED S.—There are three gangs out now; but I think we had better have some boys down on the Knoxville pike—you know we saw some Yanks there to-day. Sam, you and Tom take four or five of the boys out there by the horses, and go down near the pike and stay there until I signal for you. Joe and I will stay here and take care of the gal. [Exit Sam and Tom.] Now Joe take something to keep your courage up.

Steel drinks, Joe refuses—Steel begins to stagger as if drunk.

FRED S.—Now we will hide behind these trees until she gets here. Then I will come out and make my business known. If she refuses, I will signal you, and you can rush out behind her, stop her mouth, and then we can manage her as we please. [Exit all at R.]

Enter Alice at L.

ALICE.—This must be the place. No one here—I am not late. Can it be possible that I am deceived? I did not like the looks of those men down by the pike, and I am afraid there is foul play intended. They did not see me, however, and do not know I am here. What shall I do? I dare not try to go back to-night, it is so far. I dare not cry for help, for fear of Guerrillas. Why did he not come as he said he would?

Fred Steel advances cautiously behind Alice—She continues talking.

If he had wanted to see me, why didn't he come to Knoxville? he knew I was there, I have written him often. Oh, what shall I do? Why is he not here?

FRED S.—My dear, I am here ready to protect you.

ALICE.—Fred Steel, you here? and have I been led from home by your fiendish plottings? Lost, lost! just as I was about to see my vision of freedom realized, you cross my path to ruin all. Why do you torment me more? Are you not human, or have you lost all but the form of man? Leave me; the very sight of you is loathesome. Your foul breath is filled with rum and treason. Go, sir, I say, before I stain my hands with blood.

FRED S.—Alice, this is the only way I could manage to meet you. I have made up my mind to marry you. Once more I ask you, will you be my wife?

ALICE.—You know better than to ask me such a question. How dare you talk so to me?

FRED S.—You talk very foolish, Miss Alice. I have a company of brave boys near by who will assist me if necessary.

ALICE.—Brave man! Forge a letter, lead me far away from friends, and then tell me that you have a company of men to make me consent to marry you. Fred Steel, if you had the whole Rebel army at your command, I would not consent. [Fred S. advances.] Don't you come near me, you drunken coward. I have a pistol, and can use it if necessary. I would shoot you as soon as I would a snake if it were not for shedding human blood.

FRED S.—Come, come, Alice, don't talk so; I don't want to hurt you.

ALICE.—Fred Steel, you need not try to frighten me, I am not at all afraid of you nor your whole gang.

FRED S.—Young lady, I have fooled with you long enough.

Whistles—Joe Blake enters at R. and seizes Alice's arms and binds them behind her.

Now, Miss Marks, as soon as my boys come in we will go to Longstreet's camp, where we shall find a chaplain. We will be married, and at once start for England.

ALICE.—Merciful heaven! is it possible·that you will stoop to such baseness? But why not? you murdered my mother, and even took the life of your own brother. Yet, Fred Steel, I never will marry you.

FRED S.--Got (hic) lots of grit, havn't you (hic)? Hope you will feel better by and by.

ALICE.—Oh! that fatal letter; why was I so deceived? Oh, God! what have I done that I should suffer so? Why persecute me more? Let me die rather than fall into the power of such a traitor.

FRED S.—Shut up your head, young lady, or I will send you after your mother.

ALICE.—Do, for mercy sake, shoot me, and not torment me more.

Enter two Guerrillas at R. with Mr. Marks a prisoner.

ALICE.—Father, father! save me.

FRED S.—Good, good! now I can carry out my plans of vengeance.

MARKS.—Once more you have me in your power; once more you are sure of my blood. But there is a God in heaven, and He will not see you prosper. Let me go to my daughter.

FRED S.—Wait a few minutes, old man, and cool off a little. Here, take something to steady your nerves. [Offers Marks his canteen.]

MARKS.—Stained with murder and treason as your soul is, you now seek comfort in rum. Detestable villain, were I free, I would kill you on the spot.

FRED S.—Boys, bind the tiger fast, and go back to your post, 1 will take care of him and his gal.

Guerrillas bind Mr. Marks, and exit at R.

FRED S.—Now, old man, one word with you, and I am done.

All of the time hereafter Steel shows signs of being drunk.

I sent for your gal to come and see me this evening, and she has embraced the opportunity, but don't care to embrace me; in fact she treats me very unbecomingly. But I am willing to let all that pass if you will make her consent to marry me. What do you say?

MARKS.—If I were not bound, you would not dare talk to me in that way. There is the girl, let her answer for herself.

FRED S.—It's all fixed up between me and the gal. We are going to Longstreet's camp in the morning and get married.

Enter Sam Smith in haste at R.

SAM S.—Hurry up, Colonel, and get out of this as soon as you can. There is a scouting party from Burnside's army coming directly this way. They will gobble us all up if we don't look out.

FRED S.—All right, Sam, get the horses saddled and have the boys ready as soon as possible. [Exit Sam at R.] Now, old man, the quickest way I can get rid of you is to blow your brains out, and then I can get along with the gal, so prepare yourself.

ALICE.—Murderer, you dare not harm him. If you shoot him, you must me.

FRED S.—Shut up, or I will fix you both.

Enter Clara at L.

CLARA.—Oh, Fred! my brother! you here, and engaged in such work? Don't injure them. If you only knew how kind Alice has been to me since mother died you would not.

FRED S.—How came you here! This is no place for you.

CLARA.—I came with Alice, to bear her company.

FRED S.—You had better go out by that house (pointing), and stay a few moments; I will come and see you soon.

CLARA.—Please let me stay with Alice ; she is my best friend.

FRED S.—Go out there and stay, I tell you. [Whistles, and enter Sam S. at R.] Sam, go with my sister out by that house, and stay till I come. [Exit Sam with Clara, she crying.] Now, old Marks, if you have anything to say, hurry up. [Points revolver at Marks.]

JOE B.—(Pulling off false whiskers and hair) Fred Steel, you dare not shoot that man.

FRED S.—Walter Greenwood! how came you here? [Points revolver at Greenwood's head.] What, traitor in disguise? Die then. [Snaps cap.] Who has been tampering with my pistol? [Draws knife and rushes at Greenwood.]

WALTER G.—Fred Steel, your career of infamy is at an end. Die like the dog that you are. [Fires.) Blood streak seen from Steel's forehead to his cheek—He falls.

WALTER G.—(Kneeling to Alice) Alice, dear, forgive me; it was I who wrote that letter. It was the only way I could see to get Fred Steel and his gang within reach of our men. They are coming now. Your brother is with them.

Steel staggers to his feet.

FRED S.—Come on, boys, come on; here is old Marks' house; kill him; no, let him be; see the old woman; she has got blood on her face ; she is coming this way; go back, don't, don't touch me; see your blood is on my hands.   Oh, kill those snakes, kill them ; I can't do anything, my hands are slimy with blood ; don't let John come any nearer, he wants to kill me. See the snakes, there ; he is going to jump ; don't desert me, boys ; why don't you help me?   Go back, old woman, you have followed me long enough, let me be.   Oh, where can I go ? I can't get away ; see, the demons are about me ; they are trying to carry me off ; don't touch me.   Boys, boys, why don't you help, help ! help?   Go away; see Satan has got me by the throat; take him off; get the blood off my hands.   (Falls heavily.)

Wm. Marks and other Union soldiers rush in—All give thanks. Tableaux.

ACT IV.

Camp Scene.

COL. BARKER.—The time has arrived, boys, when you are to be free of the United States service, and this is our last day in camp. So enjoy yourselves as best you can; we are not at the front, and no fear of a surprise.

PAT. O'D.—Faith, and why didn't yes tell me that two years ago?

COL. B.—A good deal has been accomplished in that time, Patrick. We could not spare a man then, so have a good time now. We shall soon get our discharge papers, and in the morning we will be off for home.

SAM HANNIBAL.—Guess I won't go home; day don want to see me down to Knoxville. I think I will stay Norf. I helped quelch dis heah rebellion, and I's free now, and I think I better stay free.

PAT.—How the divil are ye a going to git a livin' up here? Ye betther go back.

SAM.—How I gwine to lib up heah? Why I's gwine to eat, mostly. How you git a libin?

PAT.—Why work man, and earn money.

SAM.—I'd ruver run for de Congress, den I can eat and not work.

Robert Davis.—Come, come, Patrick, let Sam be. I want to see him dance a little.

All the boys say, "Yes, Sam dance, we want to see you dance once more"—Sam dances.

Robert D.—There, Patrick, don't you wish you could do that?

Pat.—Faith and I can ; but do ye think I'd stoop so low as to dance for private soldiers?

Robert D.—Do something, Patrick, either sing a song, dan.e, or do something to keep up with Sam.

Pat sings, dances, or makes a speech.

Pat.—Bate that if ye can, and then I will try again.

All the soldiers say, "Good, good, give us some more

Capt. Dunbar.—Col., I should think Marks and Greenwood would be back soon. You know the Adjutant General said the discharges were all made out ready for the regiment.

Col. B.—I was thinking of that, Captain, and they must be here soon. But I suppose Greenwood had to step in and see Miss Marks a few minutes. You know he has been here only a week, and hasn't seen her more than fifty or sixty times. But Greenwood has been a faithful soldier, and I think it was a very wise idea to have Miss Marks come North.

Capt. D.—Walter Greenwood is every inch a soldier. I love him as a brother, and I must confess, Colonel; that it is hard for me to part with him. But to.night is our last, and I wish he would come, for I want to talk with him. By the way, Colonel, did you know that Walter was going to marry Miss Marks as soon as he is mustered out?

Col. B.—Yes, Captain, and I was in hopes he would conclude to be married to-day, so we could attend the wedding.

Enter Walter Greenwood and Mr. Marks at L.

Walter G.—Colonel, I am a little late, but I believe a satisfactory explanation can be given. Mr. Marks went with me to the Adjutant General's office, and you know I always like to tell big stories, so I told him about Mr. Marks' adventures during the war, giving him a detailed account of what he had done, what he had suffered, what he had lost; how his family had been murdered—all about it. The General asked us to wait a few minutes, when he gave Mr. Marks a beautiful letter of commendation. I tell you, Colonel, it paid for waiting.

Col. B.—Yes, Greenwood, you are entirely excusable. And the General has only done Mr. Marks justice; he deserves it all.

Walter G.—Colonel, I will return soon. [Exit L.]

Marks.—Colonel, I ask for no words of praise. If I have been of any help in crushing this rebellion, I shall receive my reward day by day. Colonel, here are the discharge papers. [Hands Col. a package.]

Col. B.—Thanks, Mr. Marks; I almost hate to take them, for they are the instruments which will sever our band, and separate us for life. We shall see each other, but never again be united as a regiment. Adjutant, please give these to the men.

Adjutant takes papers and gives each man an envelope.

Sam.—Massa Adjtint, hab you done gone forgot all about dis chile? I tink I might hab a paper, too.

Adj't.—Sam, you are not an enlisted soldier, although you have been faithful to every trust, and

Mr. Marks tells me that you were of great service to him in East Tennessee. You have much to feel proud of. Sam, you are now free. You will never be a slave any more. You can go and come where you please, and all the money you now earn is your own, and you have no master to take it away from you.

SAM.—Massa Adj't, den I can earn money and buy farder and mudder from ole Massa Brown.

ADJ'T.—Sam, your father and mother are free. Every slave in the South is free, and can now enjoy the same rights their masters do.

SAM.—I golly, is dat so, Massa Adj't, every slave in de Souf free, den who am I? I used to be Mr. Samuel Hannibal Napoleon Bonaparte Julius Cæsar Brown, Esq.; but now I done gone loss my maiden name—who is I?

ADJ'T.—That is rather a difficult question, Sam, and I think the best thing for you to do is to give up part of that name, and call yourself hereafter Mr. Samuel Brown.

SAM.—Massa, how can I call myself Brown when I's black?

ADJ'T.—O, that is your name that is all.

PAT.—Samuel, would yes be after torminting the life out of the Adjitint? Didn't I tell yes a long time ago that yes was free? and I was in for the war? Now I have got my character in black and white, showing that the colored troops is all free entirely.

MARKS.—Colonel, I have one more request to make of you. We are now citizens, but I feel that we are under your command until we break camp.

Col. B.—Any reasonable request of your's shall be granted, if in my power.

Marks.—Colonel, I have been with your regiment only a part of its term of service, but I have learned to love every man in it. By a kind providence your regiment was instrumental in delivering my only daughter from the jaws of the secession serpent, also in saving my life. Capt. Greenwood has made an arrangement with my daughter during the past week which will soon terminate in their marriage. My request, Colonel, is that they be married here in camp.

Col. B.—The very desire of my heart, my dear sir. I have not seen Miss Alice since the night she was rescued from the Guerrillas, and never have had the pleasure of her acquaintance.

Marks.—I will at once go see her, and, if I can, persuade her to come. I shall soon return. [Exit.]

Enter Mr. Marks, Walter Greenwood and Miss Alice Marks.

Marks.—Officers and men, please allow me to introduce my daughter, Alice.

All salute Miss Marks.

Col. B.—Comrades, we are about to separate and return to our homes. There we shall find happy friends to meet us. Once more we are to engage in the pursuits of civil life. We are comparatively few of the brave boys who first went to the front. Where are the rest? Some are sleeping their last sleep on Southern soil where they fell in battle; others are sleeping beneath the very shadow of the prison pens where they have died by inches; some have returned home maimed for life, and others have died of disease. We have much for which to be thankful, and as we go from here we must carry it deeply impressed upon our hearts, and be as valient in peace as we have been in war.

Marks.—Comrades, I have much that I wish to say, but I will not take up your time. I have lived to see this happy day—lived to see my children safe from the very jaws of death; lived to see the North and South again united. (Taking Alice's and Greenwood's hands.) Walter Greenwood, I freely give you my daughter's hand. Be true and faithful to her; and as the North and South have been united by fire and blood, so may you be united by the fire of love and affection, constantly thinking of Him who gave his blood for us all, and who proclaimed to the whole world: "Peace on earth; good-will toward man."

Alice.—Officers and soldiers, I can only thank you for your timely help to me on that dreadful night when I was about to suffer even worse than death. You have all suffered much in this terrible rebellion; but do not think that all of the people South were traitors to the dear old flag which now so proudly floats throughout the entire Union. Far from it; many, very many have died because of their loyalty. And as you return to your homes carry with you sympathy for them all, and remember with pride the Loyal Mountaineers of East Tennessee!

Tableaux—Curtain.